CHURCH

OPERATIONS
SECURITY (OPSEC)

BY WILLIAM SPRUCE

William Spruce
PO Box 3166
Grapevine, TX 76099

Library of Congress Cataloging in Publication Data

Original Title:

HANDBOOK
FOR
CHURCH EMERGENCY EVACUATION
AND
CHURCH EMERGENCY RESPONSE

by William Spruce

Printed in the United States of America

My people are destroyed for lack of knowledge...

Hosea 4:6
New King James Version (NKJV)

Contents

Part I - Emergency Evacuation and Fire Evacuation Procedures

Part II - Emergency Response Guidelines

Foreword

This book is written for church leaders and volunteers who provide safety for their churches and outreach locations. The information in this book is intended to assist church leaders in providing a safe environment for their members and guests. People are the most valuable asset of any church and church leaders have a responsibility to provide for their safety.

Church leaders and safety personnel should partner with their local police and fire departments to stay informed about current threats and to develop an understanding of their response capabilities.

Due to variations in church sizes, locations, and leadership the information in this book is a *general guide* for church safety. This book does not replace formal training nor the vital importance of each church developing their own standard operating procedures in the event of an emergency.

This book is a result of research I conducted to assist my local church in safety planning. The information in this guide was researched and collected from numerous common knowledge sources including governmental agencies, educational institutions, and from my own expertise after twenty-eight years in state and federal law enforcement. I use customary terminology in this book which is consistent with most evacuation plans, and response plans used by federal and state agencies. I have made a serious effort to provide accurate information in this book. However, some errors or misprints may occur.

I would like to express my appreciation to any source of information not properly acknowledged and I express my gratitude for those contributions.

William Spruce

Introduction

The promotion of personal safety and the reduction of disruption during a crisis is the primary reason each church should create an emergency plan. In any work environment or at any location where people assemble things are going to happen which involve safety and health issues.

A plan provides leaders with guidance during an emergency. Developing a plan is vital to the church because during the planning process it may lead to finding unrecognized hazardous conditions and other deficiencies.

Implementing the plan during a crisis enables the church leaders, staff, and volunteers to have a ready manual that provides a series of actions to manage an emergency until it is resolved or until first responders arrive to assume responsibility.

In a crisis the best trained responders have difficulty remembering some of the actions they need to take. This book is designed to jog the memory, so an immediate response can be taken even before first responders arrive.

Part I - EMERGENCY EVACUATION AND FIRE EVACUATION PROCEDURES

> ## OBJECTIVE 1
>
> ## PROMOTE SAFETY AND REDUCE DISRUPTION FROM CRISIS

1. Responsibilities

In case of a major disaster or crisis on any church property, defined roles and detailed instructions should be communicated to designated church leaders, volunteers, and members. Church leaders and volunteers at all levels should ensure that people in their area of control are safely evacuated.

1.1 All church staff and volunteers are responsible for knowing appropriate emergency information for their work areas and classrooms. This includes emergency plans, exits, alternate exits, and the location of fire alarm pull stations and external assembly areas.

1.2 Always follow posted **EXIT** signage to safely evacuate any building.

1.3   Emergency evacuation plan placards should be posted in prominently traveled areas. These diagrams should provide church building occupants with a primary and alternate path of exit. Copies of the emergency evacuation plans should be maintained by the administrative offices and/or the facilities management group.

2. Building Features

2.1 One of the most important building features are the primary and alternate exit paths. Follow the red or green **EXIT** signs, which always direct you to the stairwell or to the exterior of any building.

2.2   Staff and volunteers should be familiar with the alarm systems in the building. Alarms normally consist of horns, voice messages, and/or strobe lights.

2.3 Understand how the fire alarm system can be activated. Can it be manually activated at pull stations? Pull stations are normally located near the exit doors.

3. Emergency Procedures

3.1 The first person to become aware of a fire or other emergency should activate the fire alarm and then telephone **911**.

3.2 When an alarm signals on your floor, evacuate the building immediately. Follow the path designated by **EXIT** signs. *DO NOT USE THE ELEVATOR* in a building under alarm conditions, unless directed to do so by an emergency responder. Stairwells are designed to provide areas of refuge within the building and to provide safe exit from the building.

3.3 Classroom instructors are expected to interrupt class activity and instruct students to evacuate the building when the alarm activates. Staff, volunteers, and other occupants are obligated to follow emergency procedures and obey the directions of emergency response personnel.

3.4 Upon exiting the building, it is important to move as far away from the building as possible and proceed to the **pre-determined assembly areas** identified for the building. This reduces your exposure to hazardous conditions, allows for others to safely exit, and provides a clear area for emergency responders to do their job. Do not attempt to re-enter the building until emergency fire and police personnel give the "all clear" signal.

4. Individuals Requiring Assistance

4.1 Individuals who are not capable of complying with the evacuation plan, or who may have special needs or recognized disabilities should notify their church for development of an individual evacuation plan.

4.2 Occupants should be alert to the presence of persons requiring assistance to the exterior or the stairwells. Anyone who is aware of an individual needing assistance during an emergency should dial **911** and provide the name and location of the person needing assistance.

4.3 Should there be a question about interpretation of the *Americans with Disabilities Act of 1990 (ADA)*, or the church facilities, please consult church leaders.

Information on the ADA may be found at the following website:
http://www.ada.gov/pubs/ada.htm

4.4   The Center for Disability Issues and the Health Professions (CDIHP) website also features information about people with disabilities and other activity limitations. It can be viewed or downloaded from the following website:
http://www.cdihp.org/evacuation/emergency_eva cuation.pdf

5. Assembly Areas

Evacuation assembly areas outside a building should be pre-identified and marked to provide a location for evacuees to quickly gather upon exiting the building. Evacuees should follow the direction of emergency response personnel to the appropriate assembly area.

> **Assembly areas for evacuation from a building should be in an area away from the glass widows of a building to avoid any potential flying glass from the structure.**

6. *Specific Fire Emergency and Evacuation Procedures*

6.1 If You Discover a Fire:

a. Alert anyone in immediate danger.

b. Close the door to contain smoke or fire.

c. Activate the nearest fire alarm pull station.

d. If a door is hot, do not open it. There may be fire on the other side.

e. Call **911** from a safe area to provide additional information regarding the emergency.

f. Only use a fire extinguisher if the fire is small and you have been trained in the proper use of an extinguisher.

g. Evacuate the building by designated stairwells and exterior exit doors. **DO NOT USE THE ELEVATORS.**

h. Proceed to an assembly point away from the building and plaza areas. Do not re-enter the building until the "all clear" signal is given.

6.2 *If Significant Smoke, Heat, or Fire is Present:*

i. If there is smoke, stay low to the ground where cooler and cleaner air is located. If the primary exit or stairway is blocked or smoke filled, use the alternate evacuation route as shown on the emergency evacuation plan for each building.

j. If for any reason you cannot safely exit the room or building, place any available material (shirt, jacket, towel) at the bottom of the door to help seal it from smoke. If water is available, the material should be completely soaked.

k. Call **911** to inform fire and police.

l. If materials are available, a sign drawing attention to your location should be placed in the window.

m. If there are no outside signs of smoke or fire.

n. the window can be partially opened to allow waving or placement of a signal for emergency responders.

6.3 Decision to Re-Occupy:

Following an evacuation, the director of safety or safety coordinator will decide when the building will be re-occupied. If the police or fire department responded and assumed control, they normally will only release the area or building when it is declared safe.

EMERGENCY RESPONSE GUIDELINES

OBJECTIVE 2

IMPLEMENT THE ACTION PLAN TO MANAGE THE CRISIS

7. Managing the Emergency:

The key to emergency planning is to have an organized team to manage the emergency. The responsibility of the team is to help and direct others within the context of the team's ability. The objectives are to protect the people in the facility and to minimize any loss.

7.1 Director of Safety or Safety Coordinator:

The assigned safety coordinator should be very knowledgeable of the floor plans of each building and the emergency evacuation procedures for any emergency - medical, fire, tornado, etc.

The safety official will also assume the position of Incident Coordinator (IC) and has full responsibility for implementing the church emergency plan during crisis incidents by providing leadership until trained emergency fire and police arrive. The IC will report emergency response information to his/her assigned church leader who will be responsible for keeping other church leadership informed.

Responsibilities of the IC include the following:

- Coordinates emergency activities.
- Relays information during a crisis to the emergency agency (e.g., fire department, police, paramedics, emergency management, etc.)
- Coordinates with the emergency agency as needed.
- Communicates ongoing crisis information to church leadership.
- Ensures that all emergency response team members are assigned duties and follow the emergency plan.
- Works with other emergency response team members to evaluate an emergency.
- Ensures all emergency response team members have been equipped with a ball cap, jacket, or arm band to be properly identified by local or state authority arriving at the location.

The incident coordinator may also be called upon by the emergency responders to aid in crowd control and building evacuation.

7.2 Emergency Response Team Members:

Emergency response team members are staff members, teachers, safety unit members, ushers, and volunteers who are trained in evacuation techniques and use of fire extinguishers. Emergency response team members should know the location of approved assembly areas and tornado assembly areas in the building. Responsibilities of team members may include:

- Building evacuation
- Reporting to the incident coordinator that their assigned section has been cleared during an evacuation.
- If available, maintain hand-held radios to coordinate with the incident coordinator or other team members.
- Emergency response team members should immediately identify themselves as such to professional responders from local or state authority arriving at the location.

7.3 Medical Response Team Members

Medical response team members are members of the emergency response team who have been trained in medical emergencies. Their responsibilities are as follows:

- Provide basic first aid to anyone requiring medical attention until medical personnel from local or state authority assume medical treatment.
- Conducts primary assessment of medical emergencies and reports their assessment to the appropriate authority.

Be prepared to give the following information to local and state responders.

- Name, address, and telephone number
- Location of emergency
- Number of people involved
- Nature of injury or illness

8. Building Emergency Procedures

8.1 Media Inquiries

All official church statements or information communicated to the media should be coordinated with a single assigned church leader who will provide a clear message from the church to the public.

8.2 Church Leadership Responsibilities

Leader's responsibilities in an emergency include the following information and procedures:

- How to correctly respond to and summon help for a medical emergency.
- How to correctly report a fire or smoke emergency using the **911** emergency number.
- Know the location of the manual fire alarm pull stations in their area.
- Know the location of fire extinguishers and how to use a fire extinguisher.
- Know how to correctly respond to a fire warning alarm.
- Know where to assemble people during severe weather and tornados.

- Know location of primary and alternate exits and how to correctly respond to a call for an evacuation.
- Insure all opened doors are closed as areas are evacuated.

9. *Communications*

Communication is essential to the handling of any emergency. During a crisis it is important that communication lines remain available. Use telephones only when necessary to give or receive appropriate information. Church safety personnel should use hand held radios, if available, and mobile phones to assist with communications. If hand held radios are not available mobile phone group texting is an option for communicating to a group of security staff.

10. Immediate Action Situations

10.1 *ACTIVE SHOOTER*
<u>RUN</u>   <u>HIDE</u>   <u>FIGHT</u>

a) **If there is a way to escape, RUN!**
b) **RUN!** whether others do or not.
c) Leave your belongings and **RUN!**

d) Help or encourage others to **RUN!**

e) Warn others not to enter area you left.

f) Immediately call **911** and fully describe the emergency.

g) Be able to describe your location, if you fail to adequately describe your position, critical time may be lost if responders are directed to the wrong place or building.

h) Stay on the line until you are told by the **911** operator it is "ok" to hang up because there may be other critical information you will be asked to provide.

i) **HIDE!** If you are in an office, classroom, or other room with no path to run. **Close and lock the door, turn off the lights, and HIDE in a location not visible from the door or window. BE Quiet!**

j) Objects that provide protection from bullets are best to **Hide** behind.

k) Do not huddle together in one group—small groups should occupy separate locations in the room to make it more difficult for a shooter to target everyone.

l) **Prepare to Fight! for your life.** Defend yourselves in any way possible, including using any available heavy objects or sharp objects as a weapon.

m) Remain hidden until an all clear signal is given by police or proper authority.

n) Obey the commands of police authority.

> ➤ Do not approach police officers—keep your position and obey their commands.
> ➤ Always keep your hands open and visible to police officers.
> ➤ Remember that police officers may not immediately know who are victims and who are suspects.

10.2 Bomb Threat

Decision Time: Church staff or security must be ready to make a call!

a. Ignore the threat
b. Evacuate immediately (Partially or Fully)
c. Search the building and evacuate if necessary
d. Do not touch or disturb any suspicious objects

If you receive a bomb threat by telephone, illicit as much information as possible from the caller including description of bomb, detonation time; the floor and location of the bomb; the type and size; why was it placed in the building, and any information on the caller's voice - male, female, any other voice characteristics, and any background noises.

1) Report any bomb threat (or suspicious activities or objects) to church leaders or uniformed security officers and follow their instructions.
2) If you observe a search or you are told of a bomb threat, remain calm and obey instructions by security staff or first responders.
3) If an evacuation is deemed necessary and the alarm system sounds, immediately initiate evacuation procedures.
4) Direct everyone to take with them their personal items such as purses, coats, book, bags, so these items will not have to be examined and cleared during the subsequent bomb search.

10.3 Bomb Explosion

a. If a bomb explodes on an occupied floor without warning, immediately evacuate.
b. The emergency evacuation for an explosion is the same as for a fire. Immediately evacuate those able to leave the building without assistance.

c. Dial **911** and provide information about the explosion, location, and if known, the number and extent of injuries of any victims. Stay on the line until you are told by the **911** operator it is "ok" to hang up because there may be other critical information you will be asked to provide.

d. Provide any information you can to first responders about possible structural damage to the building.

10.4 Civil Disturbance

a. Churches may be a target for disruptive actions. Actions may include criminal activity like theft, burglary, robbery, assault, criminal mischief, arson, and other disruptive actions.

b. Immediately contact church staff or uniform security to report and relay suspicious activity.

c. If you are inside, remain there and secure your immediate area by locking your classroom or office door.

d. Do not over react and avoid confrontation, if possible.

e. **Defend yourself if necessary.**

f. Do not leave the building unless directed to evacuate.

g. Continue normal operations if possible.

10.5 Earthquake

DROP   **COVER**   **HOLD-ON**

a. **DROP** where you are, to your hands and knees. (This position prevents you from being knocked down and also allows you to stay low for crawling to a desk, table or chair for shelter.)

b. **COVER** your head and neck with an arm and use the other hand and arm to **HOLD ON** to something sturdy. If no shelter is nearby, crawl next to an interior wall (away from windows).

c. Stay on your knees; bend over to protect vital organs and **HOLD ON** until the shaking stops. If under shelter hold on to the shelter with one hand and be ready to move with your shelter if it shifts or moves.

d. **Cover** your head and neck with both arms and hands if you have no shelter.

e. Instruct others to stay under cover (such as a desks, tables, or doorways); move away from the windows, bookcases, etc., to avoid falling debris.

f. Immediately call **911** describing the emergency situation.

g. Remain calm and wait for instructions of emergency responders.

h. If communications are out and it becomes evident that the building is unstable and is unsafe, initiate an evacuation. Be alert as all occupants may be evacuating the building at the same time, so it may take longer to clear the building.

i. **Do not use elevators,** assist others who may need help, and be patient.

j. Be ready for aftershocks.

k. Treat or assist injured people with first aid and CPR as needed depending on your level of expertise.

l. First aid may have to be administered to the injured until they can be attended to by trained medical professionals or transported to a hospital for treatment.

m. Don't move victims unless they are in immediate danger. If necessary, put out small fires with portable fire extinguishers.

n. Avoid areas where structural damage may have rendered the building unsafe. Wait in a safe place for instructions.

o. Expect delays in emergency response services.

p. Expect fire alarms and other protection systems to activate.

q. Do not flush toilets because sewer lines may not be intact.

10.6 *Fire*

a. Immediately activate the nearest fire alarm station and evacuate everyone on your floor.
b. Dial **911** and provide specific information about the fire, including the extent of any casualties.
c. Direct people to the assembly areas and remain there until further instructions are given by police or fire personnel.

10.7 Flooding

a. If flooding occurs within a building it may be caused by internal factors such as plumbing problems, or external sources related to weather. A quick response can prevent extensive damage to the property.
b. Electrical power and natural gas or propane tanks should be shut off to avoid electrocution or fire after a premise is flooded. Electrical and gas/propane systems should be checked for safety before they are turned on.
c. Notify a church leader and provide as much information as possible about the flooding source.
d. Act immediately to limit water damage. Move equipment and furniture as required, turn off and cover computers and other sensitive

equipment with plastic sheeting, and assist with protecting any vital records, information, and other items.

10.8 Hazardous Materials Incident

a. Do not approach the spill.
b. Call **911** to provide necessary information and follow their instructions.
c. If the spill is outside of the building, remain inside the building until conditions allow for the safe evacuation of the area.
d. If the spill is inside the building, isolate and evacuate the affected area immediately.
e. If the size or effect of the spill warrants, activate the fire alarm and initiate a floor evacuation.
f. Help keep others out of the area until help arrives.

10.9 Power Outage

a. Notify a church leader to report an outage.
b. In the event of a total or near-total loss of power to the building, it is essential for all building occupants to remain calm, especially if it is late evening or night.
c. Offer reassurance to others in your area.

d. Most churches are equipped with lighting fixtures that will provide reduced emergency lighting for several hours permitting safe evacuation if it becomes necessary.
e. Telephones and computers will not normally operate during a general power outage.
f. Be sure to conduct a thorough search of your floor to ensure that everyone has left the building before it is secured.

10.10 Severe Weather

a. If conditions such as a major winter storm or other severe weather conditions warrant the closure of the church then a designated church leader should notify the staff and members of the suspension of normal operations, including any cancellation of services.
b. In the event of potentially destructive weather, such as dangerously high wind conditions, occupants will be warned to move to an interior location of the building.

Assembly areas should be away from external windows, doors, and walls. Interior offices or rooms are ideal for gathering people.

10.11 Threatening Person

a. Do not confront or argue with people who are behaving in a threatening manner.
b. Immediately notify church staff, uniform security, or police providing the exact location and a description of the subject.
c. Encourage others to avoid the immediate area.

10.12 Threatening Phone Call

a. Ask the caller's identity and to whom they wish to speak.
b. Write down the telephone number and name of the caller as this information appears on the caller ID display.
c. Remain calm and do not react emotionally to anything the caller says.
d. Do not give out any information about persons the caller threatens during the call.
e. Make written notes during the conversation including the types and nature of any threats, names of persons the caller mentions, characteristics of the caller's voice, and any other information that may help identify the caller or assist during a later investigation.

f. If the caller's only purpose is to shock you with profane or abusive language or to lure you into an argument, terminate the call without comment.

g. Immediately report the call to church leadership as soon as the call is ended.

10.13 Suspicious Object

What makes an object suspicious? It is any unusual circumstances about the objects origin, someone believes it to be of suspicious origin, and that its origin has not been immediately determined.

---

*Do not touch or move the item/object!
If any object or vehicle cannot be established as non-threating then the item/object must be treated as an improvised explosive device (IED). **Call 911.**

Any church member or safety personnel should obtain the following information regarding a suspicious object or package and provide it to the responding police.

a. The person reporting the object or package.
b. Complete description of the object.
c. The exact location.
d. Has any attempt been made to hide the item?
e. The time the object/package was discovered.
f. Are there any sensitive or vulnerable areas close to object or package?
g. Have steps been taken to identify the owner?
h. Is the witness available to speak with the police?
i. Has any prominent church leader or member received any recent threats?
j. Is the date of the incident significant to the church? For example, an anniversary, etc.?
k. Has there been a specific threat or hoax threat to the location or premises?
l. Does the incident follow a recent trend of any other suspicious objects or packages?

Assessing Suspicious Objects or Packages

(**Never touch or move any suspicious item during assessment. If you are in doubt at any time with the suspected item, clear the area and Dial 911)

Interview assessment

(*If no witness begin visual and smell assessment)

> Identify person reporting the object or package
> Speak to any other witnesses to gather additional information to assess the suspicious object or package

❖ Questions to ask –

- Who and Why was witness alerted to suspect item?
- Location, time the object/package was discovered, and detailed description.
- Did you move the item? (If witness moved the item and it did not explode that is a positive indicator)
- Did you look inside the bag, box, container, etc… ? (If the witness looked inside item they may be able to describe what was inside the suspicious item)
- Do you know who the item belongs too?
- Do you have an opinion on who may have left the item?
- Have steps been taken to identify or notify the owner?

- Was there any unusual activity before the item was discovered?
- Has there been a specific threat or any hoax threat to this location or to any person at the location?
- Have there been any other suspicious objects or packages left at this location?
- Is anyone at this location having relationship problems or martial problems?
- If business, what type of business?

Visual and smell assessment
(Observations below are **red flags, Dial 911)

- ➢ Does the item require to be moved before entering a door, a hallway, a sidewalk, a driveway, or road?
- ➢ Anything unusual about location of the suspect item?
- ➢ Are there any sensitive or vulnerable areas close to object or package? Structures, Utilities, government offices, large crowds..
- ➢ Has the object been hidden or disguised?
- ➢ Any wet or oily stains present on exterior of object or packages? (may indicate explosives sweating)

- Any white/gray colored granules/powder present on exterior of object or packages? (may indicate homemade explosives)
- Are there any visible wires on exterior of object or package?
- Lopsided or usual shape
- Any strange odors associated with the item?

(Unusual fumes causing headaches, dizziness, chest pain, and/or low blood pressure. **Homemade explosives and nitroglycerin based explosives may emit fumes that are pungent and sensitive to smell)

Assessing Suspicious Letters or Packages

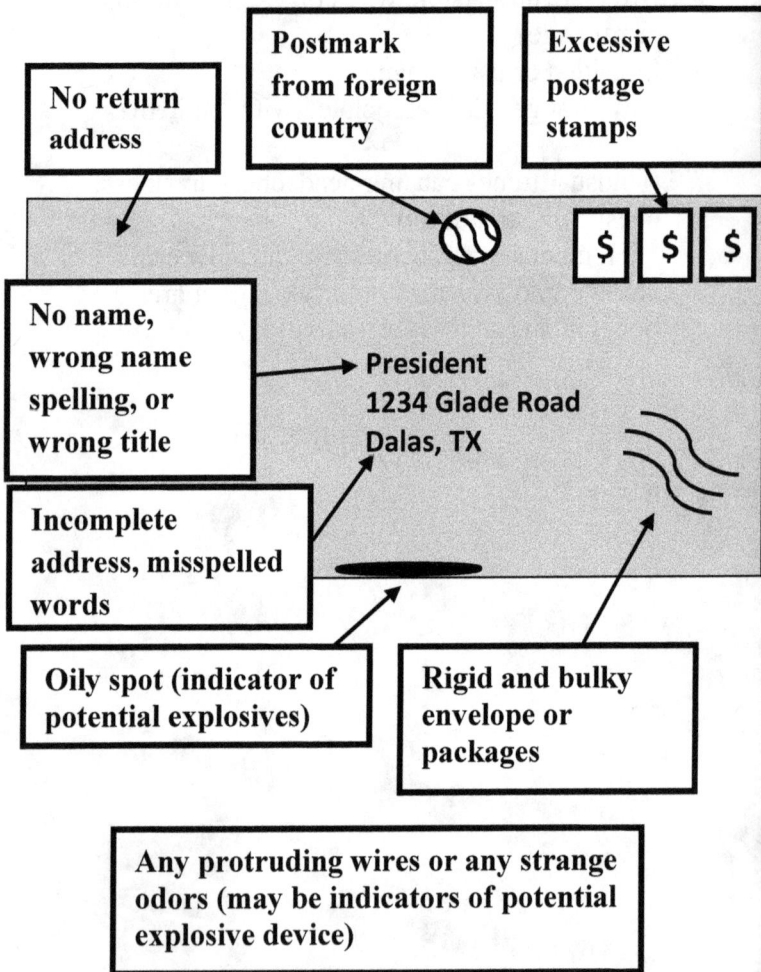

No return address

Postmark from foreign country

Excessive postage stamps

$ $ $

No name, wrong name spelling, or wrong title

President
1234 Glade Road
Dalas, TX

Incomplete address, misspelled words

Oily spot (indicator of potential explosives)

Rigid and bulky envelope or packages

Any protruding wires or any strange odors (may be indicators of potential explosive device)

Assessing Suspicious Vehicles

a. Be able to describe the vehicle (color, make model, approximate age, license plate, etc.)
b. Exact location
c. Can anything unusual be seen in the vehicle?
d. Is the vehicle sagging as if it has something heavy inside?
e. Does the vehicle have any signs of structural changes?
f. Do the locks on the doors and trunk appear to be in tact or have they been damaged or removed?
_g._ Are there any wires protruding from any opening in the vehicle?

---

* If the suspicious vehicle is occupied it is best to notify the police and do not approach the vehicle.

Recommended Plan Diagrams

A diagram should be posted on each floor, and minimally contain the following information:

* Location of fire alarms
* Location of fire extinguishers
* Exit routes from the floor
* Location of emergency exits
* Exterior assembly areas
* Location(s) of Automated External Defibrillator (AED)

www.ingramcontent.com/pod-product-compliance
Lightning Source LLC
Chambersburg PA
CBHW060702280326
41933CB00012B/2276